DHEA

The Youth and Health Hormone

Its promise as an
antidote to the diseases
of aging and as a whole-
body rejuvenator

C. Norman Shealy, M.D., Ph.D.

Keats Publishing, Inc.   New Canaan, Connecticut

ABOUT THE AUTHOR

C. Norman Shealy, M.D. is founder and director of The Shealy Institute for Comprehensive Health Care in Springfield, Missouri, the first multimodal pain rehabilitation center of its kind. His many medical innovations include the introduction of the concept of transcutaneous electrical nerve stimulation (TENS) and the first biofeedback training program for chronic pain which he introduced in 1972. Dr. Shealy organized and was the founding president of the American Holistic Medical Association. He is the author of many books including the widely acclaimed *The Creation of Health* (with Carolyn Myss). His most recent book is *Miracles Do Happen*.

The research presented in this work was supported by a grant from the Life Science Foundation.

DHEA is not intended as medical advice. Its intent is solely informational and educational. Please consult a health professional should the need for one be indicated.

ISBN: 0-87983-695-4

Printed in the United States of America

Good Health Guides are published by
Keats Publishing, Inc.
27 Pine Street (Box 876)
New Canaan, Connecticut 06840-0876

CONTENTS

THE DHEA PATHWAY

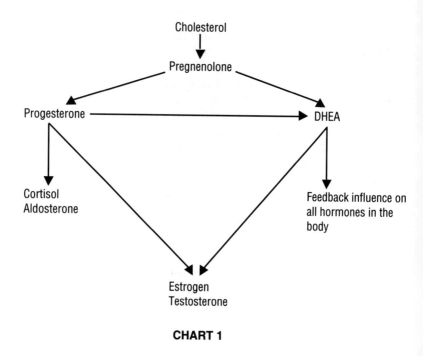

Cholesterol

Pregnenolone

Progesterone

DHEA

Cortisol
Aldosterone

Feedback influence on
all hormones in the
body

Estrogen
Testosterone

CHART 1

DHEA or dehydroepiandrosterone, the most abundant hormone in humans and mammals, is an essential component in many physiological functions. It plays a major role in the immune system; it is a building block for sexual and other hormones; and it determines general levels of well-being and mood. Although we have known about DHEA for almost 50 years, there have been relatively few clinical studies until the last decade. However, research shows that DHEA may be the most critical single chemical in the body in predicting disease or health.

DHEA is deficient in every major disease, including obesity, diabetes, high blood pressure, cancer, various immune deficiencies, coronary artery disease and autoimmune disorders. Oral replacement of DHEA appears to be of benefit in all of these illnesses with no significant reported complications. On the other hand, natural enhancement of DHEA levels is now feasible and at least from a theoretical point of view, much more desirable.

DHEA is manufactured in the body from cholesterol; yet it is interesting to note that DHEA levels often decline with aging while cholesterol levels increase. This fact leads to speculation that there may be some enzymatic process that fails during adulthood. Ordinarily the manufacture of DHEA in the body proceeds as shown in Chart 1. It is worth noting that the first major hormone manufactured from cholesterol is pregnenolone and from pregnenolone we make both progesterone and DHEA. Generally progesterone proceeds in its metabolic pathway toward the production of cortisol or aldosterone, as well as to estrogen and testosterone. Cortisol is the major adrenal stress hormone and aldosterone is the major adrenal hormone for mineral balance; but progesterone is also a precursor for estrogen and testosterone. DHEA is also used to make testosterone and estrogen and it serves as well as a major regulator in a feedback mechanism on all other hormones in the body, including the thyroid and pituitary itself.

It is interesting to note that both the progesterone and the DHEA pathways lead to production of testosterone and estrogen. In women after menopause, many symptoms are caused by deficiencies of progesterone and most menopausal symptoms can be treated by giving natural progesterone. Furthermore, throughout adulthood men actually produce more estrogen than postmenopausal women.

The Stress Response

One major metabolic effect of DHEA is its involvement in glucose metabolism. The glucose and glucocorticoid (cortisol) feedback inhibition loop is the key factor determining the intensity and duration of the stress reaction. One of the feedback inhibition loops that cortisol is involved in is with the hypothalamus, the regulator of body function, which has a feedback and inhibition relationship with cortisol. When blood cortisol decreases, the hypothalamus releases corticotrophic releasing hormone (CRF) which in turn releases ACTH which stimulates the adrenal cortex to release cortisol.

Obviously the stress response is much more complex than just that of cortisol and its feedback mechanism. Interestingly, there is also a relationship between cortisol and DHEA in a feedback loop mechanism. Perhaps one of the least understood and recognized aspects of stress is that stress includes physical, chemical, emotional and electromagnetic factors. The major stressors follow:

PHYSICAL	**CHEMICAL**
• Inactivity	• Sugar
• Toxins	• Infection
• Inadequate light	• Nutrition imbalance
• Allergens	• Nicotine
• Temperature extremes	• Caffeine
• Trauma	• Alcohol

EMOTIONAL	**ELECTROMAGNETIC**
• Fear	• Automobiles
• Anger	• Refrigerators
• Guilt	• Television
• Anxiety	• Computers
• Depression	• Computer printers
• Pain	• Airplanes
• Inadequate sleep	• Fluorescent lights

The effects of these stressors are ordinarily handled in the body by a normal balancing mechanism called homeostasis. This is demonstrated in Chart 2. This is the normal stress response which Hans Selye called an alarm reaction. However, if stress continues, the body begins to adapt and the adaptation phase begins to produce some changes in the efficiency of the stress reaction as seen in Chart 3.

Selye has emphasized that individuals who have never been exposed to a given stressor have a marked alarm reaction. For instance, an individual who does not smoke will have a rise in norepinephrine (the precursor of adrenalin) to almost 200 percent of baseline while smoking a cigarette but if that individual continues to smoke the cigarette daily, he or she will adapt and smoking will have minimal effect upon norepinephrine. However, Selye, who has been called "the father of stress," emphasized that every time we adapt to one stressor we lower our threshold for a new stressor.[1] So, if a non-coffee-drinking individual would ordinarily require a cup of coffee to double the norepinephrine production, one who has adapted to cigarettes might require only two-thirds or half a cup of

NORMAL STRESS RESPONSE

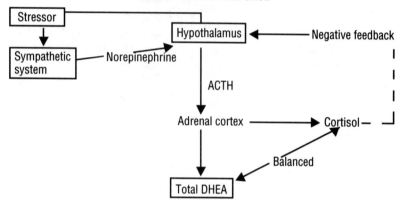

- ACTH, cortisol & DHEA are increased equally
- DHEA represents chemical stress reservoir

CHART 2

CHRONIC STRESS RESPONSE (ADAPTATION)

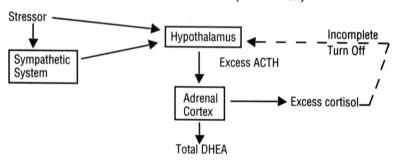

Increased cortisol
Stable DHEA
Blood sugar unstable
Osteoporosis begins
Fat deposits in body
Salt and water retention
Slight decreases in immune system

CHART 3

coffee. Thus, it continues so that by the time you have adapted to three or four stressors, or even hundreds, it may take less than half as much of a new stress to cause an alarm reaction.

Selye also emphasized that subliminal or sub-threshold, "dosages" of stress are additive. For instance, it may take one cigarette to create an alarm reaction but a third of a cigarette doesn't really trigger it. On the other hand, a third of a cigarette, a third of a cup of coffee, and perhaps two teaspoons of sugar might be capable of triggering an alarm reaction.

All of these integral interrelationships of stress are almost certainly a prime contributor ultimately to the body's loss of homeostasis and the gradual progression through the chronic stress adaptation-maladaptation-exhaustion stages. It is entirely probable that by the time you get to adaptation, it is already difficult to maintain the DHEA at its optimal levels, 750 ng/dL (nanograms per deciliter of blood) or above in men or 550 ng/dL or above in women. Certainly by the time you get to the exhaustion stage, DHEA depletion is the major finding.

THE RESULTS OF CHRONIC STRESS (EXHAUSTION)
- Cortisol increased 24 hours a day
- DHEA decreased
- Insulin erratic—excess followed by deficiencies
- Poor sleep recovery
- Immune system significantly deficient
- Major illnesses begin
    Heart disease
    Stroke
    Cancer
    Infections
    Autoimmune disorders
    Degenerative diseases

Prior to our understanding of DHEA action, the mechanism of "exhaustion" was a psychological term. Now we have chemical correlates to go with the diagnosis as shown below in Chart 4.

DHEA LEVELS AND STRESS

Serious Deficiency	Worrisome Low	Fair	Good	Excellent
Male < 180	180–349	350–599	600–749	750–1250
Female < 130	130–299	300–449	450–549	550–980
EXHAUSTION	◄—*PROGRESSIVE MALADAPTATION*		ADAP- TATION	HOMEO- STASIS
SERIOUS ILLNESS	DEGENERATION			

CHART 4

DHEA: THE KEY TO HEALTH OR DISEASE

Because conventional physicians pay little or no attention to DHEA, they are unable to find anything physically wrong in patients with a wide variety of chronic stress illnesses. The usual medical history and physical exam will generally alert the physician to suspect the most serious diagnosable illnesses such as cancer, major heart disease, brain tumors or even diabetes. But the standard screening chemical tests (a simultaneous multiple analyzer computerized biochemical profile and CBC blood count) may be "normal" even in these more serious illnesses. Regular X rays, electrocardiograms, and even very specialized X rays such as CT scans or MRI (magnetic resonance imaging) are useful when there are tumors, fractures, ruptured discs and so on.

But a significant majority of patients who seek a physician's help do not have illnesses detectable by all these excellent tests. Instead, these "undiagnosable" patients often have a wide variety of symptoms, including fatigue, anxiety, depression, dizziness, nausea, diarrhea and a wide variety of aches and pains which do not fit the common medical model.

The diagnostic dilemma is the simple fact that stress can cause every known symptom but there is no diagnostic test for stress. However, cumulative stress leads to an increasing number of symptoms. If you have 20 or more symptoms at the same time, you are likely to have a DHEA deficiency. If you have less than 10 symptoms, it is likely that your DHEA level is good or excellent. Here is a simple test to begin an analysis of your own personal reactions to stress. In the following list, check only those symptoms you have now or ones which have been significant in the past 6 months.

SYMPTOM INDEX

_____ Depressed mood
_____ Significant weight loss or gain
_____ Insomnia
_____ Oversleeping
_____ Fatigue, low energy
_____ Feelings of worthlessness or guilt
_____ Difficulty concentrating
_____ Indecisiveness
_____ Recurrent thoughts of death or suicide
_____ Nervous exhaustion
_____ Anxiety or worry
_____ Frequent crying
_____ Being extremely shy
_____ Lumps or swelling in neck
_____ Vision problems
_____ Hearing problems
_____ Motion sickness
_____ Teeth or gum problems
_____ Sore or sensitive tongue
_____ Change in sense of taste
_____ Breathing problems
_____ Frequent colds
_____ Sore throat or hoarseness
_____ Enlarged tonsils
_____ Difficulty in swallowing
_____ Coughing spells
_____ High or low blood pressure
_____ Heart problems
_____ Shortness of breath
_____ Heartburn
_____ Feeling bloated
_____ Excess belching
_____ Nausea
_____ Peptic ulcer
_____ Loss of appetite
_____ Digestive problems
_____ Excess hunger
_____ Frequent urination at night
_____ Urinary problems

_____ Constipation
_____ Diarrhea
_____ Other bowel problems
_____ Frequent stomach trouble
_____ Intestinal worms
_____ Hemorrhoids
_____ Yellow jaundice
_____ Biting your nails
_____ Stuttering or stammering
_____ Sexual problems
_____ Hernia or rupture
_____ Kidney or bladder disease
_____ Stiff or painful muscles or joints
_____ Back or shoulder pain
_____ Painful feet
_____ Swelling in armpits or groin
_____ Leg cramps
_____ Itching or burning skin
_____ Dizziness
_____ Cold hands or feet
_____ Epilepsy
_____ Tendency to shake or tremble
_____ Tendency to be too hot or too cold
_____ Sedentary
_____ Overweight or underweight
_____ Dental problems
_____ Coated tongue
_____ Varicose veins
_____ Headaches
_____ Surgery within the past year
_____ Get angry easily
_____ Feel lonely or sad

For men only:
_____ Weak or slow urine stream
_____ Prostate trouble
_____ Swelling or lumps in testicles
_____ Trouble getting erections

For women only:

_____ Difficult or heavy menses	_____ Vaginal discharge
_____ PMS	_____ Hot flashes
_____ On birth control pills (in last year)	_____ Have had a hysterectomy
_____ Lumpy breasts	_____ On hormonal replacement

Although research shows a strong correlation between chemical, physical and emotional stress and a patient's diverse symptoms, most physicians do not evaluate even the most basic and best known measure of stress—social change.[2] Almost 40 years ago, Drs. Holmes and Rahe, developers of the Social Readjustment Scale which follows, demonstrated that individuals who had significant social change within the past year had an 80 percent chance of developing illness within the subsequent year. I have found in my practice that the higher the chemical, physical and emotional stress, the greater the number of symptoms. If conventional physicians can't find any "real" illness in this situation, they are quite likely to tell you it is "all in your head." An opportunity to assess *your* total life stress follows. If you score 75 or more points and have many symptoms, but no diagnosable illness, you are well on your way to burnout and probably have a DHEA level well below optimal, most probably in the poor or serious range.

TOTAL LIFE STRESS TEST

Circle the answers appropriate for you.

I. *Chemical Stress*

Average daily sugar consumption	(total used)
Sugar added to food or drink (teaspoons)	0 1 2 3 4
Sweet roll, piece of pie/cake, brownie, other dessert (# per day)	0 1 2 3 4
Soda or candy bar (# per day)	0 1 2 3 4
Ice cream (# per day)	0 1 2 3 4
White flour (white bread, pasta, pastry, etc.—circle 2 if you use it)	2
Average daily salt consumption (how often?)	
I add salt to my food	0 1 2 3 4
I eat salty food	0 1 2 3 4
Average daily caffeine consumption (# per day?)	
Coffee	0 1 2 3 4
Tea	0 1 2 3 4

Cola drink or Mountain Dew		0 1 2 3 4
Anacin or aspirin		0 1 2 3 4
Caffeine benzoate tablets (NoDoz, Vivarin, etc.)		0 1 2 3 4
	Dietary subtotal	_____

B. *Other chemical stress* (Circle the number by each statement that applies).

Drinking water

| My water is chlorinated | 1 |
| My water is chlorinated and fluoridated | 2 |

Soil and Air Pollution

Live within 10 miles of city of 500,000 or more	4
Live within 10 miles of city of 250,000 or more	2
Live within 10 miles of city of 50,000 or more	2
Live in the country but use pesticides, herbicides, and/or chemical fertilizer	4
Exposed to cigarette smoke of someone else more than one hour per day	4

Drugs (For any amount of usage, circle 4)

Antidepressants	4
Tranquilizers	4
Sleeping pills	4
Narcotics	4
Other pain relievers	4
Marijuana or other street drugs	4
Drug subtotal	_____

Nicotine (Circle those that apply)

3–10 cigarettes per day	4
11–20 cigarettes per day	8
21–30 cigarettes per day	10
31–40 cigarettes per day	20
Over 40 cigarettes per day	40
I smoke cigars	4
I smoke a pipe	4
I use chewing tobacco	8
Nicotine subtotal	_____

Average daily alcohol consumption

1 drink = 1 oz. whiskey, gin or vodka;
        8 oz. beer or
        4–6 oz. wine

1 drink per day	2
2 drinks per day	4
3 or more drinks per day	20
Alcohol subtotal	_____

II. Physical stress
Weight (circle that which applies)

Underweight more than 10 lbs.	5
10 to 25 lbs. overweight	5
16 to 25 lbs. overweight	10
26 to 40 lbs. overweight	20
More than 40 pounds overweight	40

Activity (circle that which applies)

30 minutes of exercise, 3 days or more per week	0
Some physical exercise, 1 or 2 days per week	15
No regular exercise	40

Work stress (circle that which applies)

Sit most of the day	3
Industrial/factory worker	3
Overnight travel more than once a week	5
Work more than 50 hours per week	10
Work varying shifts	10
Work night shift	5
Heavy labor—physically fit	0
Heavy labor—not physically fit	40
Physical stress subtotal	_____

III. Attitudinal stress
A. Holmes-Rahe Social Readjustment Rating*
(Circle those events listed below which you have experienced during the past 12 months)

Death of a spouse	10
Divorce	7
Marital separation	6
Jail term	6
Death of a close family member	5
Personal injury or illness	5
Marriage	5
Fired at work	5
Marital reconciliation	5
Retirement	5
Change in health of family member	4
Pregnancy	4
Sexual difficulties	4
Gain of a new family member	4
Business readjustment	4
Change in financial state	4

*Holmes, T.H. and Rahe, R.H.: The Social Readjustment Rating Scale. *Journal of Psychosomatic Research*, 11:213–213. Reproduced with permission of the authors and publisher. Scoring adapted.

Death of close friend	4
Change to different line of work	4
Change in number of arguments with spouse	4
Mortgage over $20,000	3
Foreclosure of mortgage or loan	3
Change in responsibilities at work	3
Son or daughter leaving home	3
Trouble with in-laws	3
Outstanding personal achievement	2
Spouse begins or stops work	3
Begin or end school	3
Change in living conditions	3
Revision of personal habits	2
Trouble with boss	3
Change in work hours or condition	2
Change in residence	2
Change in schools	2
Change in recreation	2
Change in church activities	2
Change in social activities	2
Mortgage or loan less than $20,000	1
Change in eating habits	1
Vacation, especially if away from home	1
Christmas, or other major holiday stress	1
Minor violations of the law	1

Total points _____

B. *Other emotional stress* (circle those that apply)

Sleep	
Less than 7 hours per night	4
Usually 7 or 8 hours per night	0
More than 8 hours per night	2
Relaxation	
Relax only during sleep	4
Relax or meditate at least 20 minutes per day	0
Frustration at work	
Enjoy work	0
Mildly frustrated by job	1
Moderately frustrated by job	4
Very frustrated by job	8
Lack of authority at job	8
Boss doesn't trust me	8
Marital Status	
Married, happily	0

Married, moderately unhappy	4
Married, very unhappy	8
Unmarried man over 30	2
Unmarried woman over 30	1

Usual Mood

Happy, well adjusted	0
Moderately angry, depressed or frustrated	4
Very angry, depressed or frustrated	8

Overall Attitude

Degree of feeling hopeless	0 1 2 3 4
Degree of feeling depressed	0 1 2 3 4
Inability to achieve major goal	0 1 2 3 4
Inability to achieve close love/intimacy	0 1 2 3 4
Degree to which I am frustrated, annoyed, and/or angry because someone attacked or harmed me or prevented me from happiness	0 1 2 3 4

(Below, score a 0 if you agree;
score a 1, 2, 3, or 4, if you disagree)

Satisfied and in control of my life	0 1 2 3 4
Experience happiness regularly	0 1 2 3 4
Believe I am responsible for my happiness	0 1 2 3 4
Believe and experience happiness is an inside job	0 1 2 3 4
Any other major emotional stress not mentioned above. You judge intensity 0–10	_____
Other Emotional Stress Subtotal	_____
Attitudinal stress subtotal	_____

Total Life Stress

I. Chemical Total	_____
II. Physical Total	_____
III. Attitudinal Total	_____
TLS TOTAL	_____

For Scoring:
Dietary subtotal
For a score above 10, clean up your nutrition.
Drug subtotal
For a score of 4 or more, you need detoxification.
Nicotine
For any score, Stop! Nicotine blocks DHEA *Alcohol*
For a score above 6, you need alcohol control.
Physical stress subtotal
For a score of 40 or more, you desperately need exercise.

Social readjustment rating
   For a score of 30 or more, you need stress control.
Other emotional stress
   For a score of 10 or more, you need counselling or a stress management program.

If your Total Life Stress score is 100 or more, your DHEA is likely to suffer. A Total Life Stress score of 50 or less is compatible with DHEA homeostasis.

In addition to the stressors you've noted above, the following will also contribute to excess stress and eventually to adrenal exhaustion:
• Not being outside in sunshine at least one hour per day.
• Being indoors in "managed" air most of the time.
• A general sense of lack of meaning or purpose in life.

In general you can assume that if you score high on the Symptom Index, even though a physician's history, physical examination and recent laboratory tests reveal no diagnosis, you have at least partial adrenal burnout and you are likely to have a DHEA blood level well below the optimal outlined in Chart 5B. In this case DHEA supplementation is likely to be the key to solving your problem.

V.M. Dilman[3] considers excessive and prolonged increase in cortisol in response to stress and an elevated basal cortisone level to be the beginning of maladaptation to stress and he calls this particular state "hyperadaptosis." It is interesting that Prednisone, a synthetic cortisol-like chemical, has a much greater diabetogenic effect with increasing age. There is also some evidence of damage to the hippocampus (a memory center of the brain) with oral doses of cortisone and this may well take place in chronic cortisol elevation from prolonged stress.

DHEA has such diverse physiological and biochemical action that it is theorized that it has specific receptors and that at some level may even have specific DHEA binding proteins.[4]

DHEA actually has a relatively mild androgenic (male sex hormone) effect. It is remarkably free of side effects. A very small percentage of patients given DHEA may develop mild acne and, very rarely, there may be a slight increase in female facial hair with administration of DHEA.

But as I will discuss later, it is possible to restore DHEA levels without taking DHEA supplements. Indeed, I believe DHEA rejuvenation is the single most important discovery in the history of medicine.

THE DHEA-FEEDBACK COMPLEX

L-tryptophan and L-dopa both improve the sensitivities of the brain to dexamethasone suppression tests. Dexamethasone is another cortisone analog. Thus, the tryptophan/serotonin and dopamine/epinephrine systems are intimately related to DHEA metabolism. Norepinephrine stimulates the secretion of gonadotropins but it is inhibited by dopamine (a precursor of epinephrine) along one of the secretory pathways. High levels of gonadotropins (boosters for testes and ovaries) suggest higher DHEA levels. High levels of both serotonin and melatonin (a major "sleep" hormone) inhibit reproductive function. The hypothalamus is extremely sensitive to negative feedback, such as increased levels of cortisol with decreased levels of DHEA, but this sensitivity decreases in older individuals.

Similarly, free testosterone decreases with age largely because of increased binding of testosterone to globulin and lower levels of DHEA. High blood glucose levels inhibit growth hormone and low blood glucose levels stimulate growth hormone, which is theoretically good for DHEA. High blood levels of fatty acids decrease growth hormone (thus inhibiting DHEA). High carbohydrate diets prevent the increase in growth hormone which normally occurs when one ingests arginine, an amino acid found in protein. Arginine would thus be complementary to DHEA.

Growth hormone is a powerful insulin antagonist; thus it enhances DHEA. Fasting increases both growth hormone secretion and DHEA. Growth hormone is stimulated by norepinephrine (an adrenaline precursor) and serotonin, all of which also assist DHEA. Low catecholamines (adrenalin) and low levels of serotonin are seen in patients with depression, along with low DHEA. Obesity decreases growth hormone (and DHEA). Niacin is essential for production of serotonin which, as noted above, raises growth hormone.

Dilman considers the physiologic and biochemical parameters of a healthy 20 to 25-year-old to be those that we should consider "normal." Anything that decreases from those 25-year-old levels is already maladaptation and leads to major problems of aging, including cancer and atherosclerosis. Dilman recommends 5 or 6 mg of melatonin at bedtime for every individual as well as caloric restriction and physical exercise.

Gamma-aminobutyric acid (GABA), niacin and tryptophan all increase serotonin and should help increase DHEA. The amino acids tyrosine and phenylalanine increase norepinephrine and should help increase DHEA. The amino acids arginine, ornithine and lysine increase immune function and probably enhance DHEA. Dilman's is the only publication we have seen which shows a possibility of converting progesterone into DHEA.

Finally, in understanding the complex interaction of DHEA with a variety of other neurochemicals, it is important to note that DHEA is antagonistic to GABA, the major inhibitory neurochemical. Thus, due to a feedback loop, GABA is turned off as DHEA increases. Excessive GABA activity has been implicated in brain aging, brain degeneration and in Alzheimer's disease.[5] This anti-GABA activity fits well with the fact that DHEA is synergistic with norepinephrine and serotonin, both excitatory chemicals.

The very latest research indicates that young army trainees subjected to eight weeks of sleep deprivation had a greater than two-fold increase in cortisol levels, profound suppression of testosterone, marked decreases in several aspects of immune function, but slight increased levels of DHEA.[6] This is compatible with the early stages of maladaptation to stress. Almost certainly continued stress would lead to marked lowering of DHEA and to illness. The ability of younger individuals to withstand such stress is not likely to be found in the elderly.

It is now evident that administration of DHEA in the elderly leads to a four-fold increase in immune function specific to vaccine immunization.[7] In other words, older individuals who have poor immune antibody response to vaccination will produce adequate antibodies if given DHEA at the time of vaccination. DHEA in this situation "restores" a healthy immune system. DHEA protects against the brain inhibitory effects of stress, but only if given in advance of the stressful event.[8]

DRUGS AND DHEA

Propranolol, a widely used (and I believe medically abused) antihypertensive drug, should be used only in patients with significant cardiovascular disease and should never be used as a prophylactic in treating migraine or even in treating mitral valve prolapse because this ultimately leads to decreases in melatonin and almost certainly to decreases in DHEA.[9]

There are many other drugs which probably suppress DHEA; all the beta blockers and calcium channel blockers are prime suspects for adverse effects upon DHEA. It is likely that DHEA supplementation would do a far superior job of treating the diseases for which these drugs are used. Further research is certainly essential.

Insulin appears to act as a physiological regulator of DHEA metabolism and lowers DHEA levels at least in men. Thus any stress may lower DHEA since increased blood sugar is one of the essentials of the stress reaction.[10] DHEA effects a major enzyme in glucose metabolism and this in turn is important in DHEA's anti-tumor properties. Indeed, the interplay between DHEA and insulin is perhaps the key to the end effects of stress (See Chart 3B). Intravenous administration of insulin leads to acute lowering of DHEA and inhibits adrenal androgen production in men. This male dominant activity may explain the increased risk of heart disease in men with low DHEA.[11] In women, too, below optimal levels of DHEA are associated with heart disease.

DHEA AND DISEASE

DHEA levels are inversely associated with the extent of coronary artery disease; stress reduction techniques appear to improve blood levels of DHEA,[12] as well as reduce the risk of coronary artery disease. DHEA is significantly lower in patients with acute myocardial infarction,[13] the most common serious heart disease. DHEA levels are also significantly lower in patients with prostatic cancer.[14] Japanese researchers have theorized that disturbed balance between cortisol and DHEA results in various aging and stress related disorders.[15]

There is one study which found that DHEA levels do not correlate with aging alone until about 98 years of age. Although many individuals have decreases in DHEA before age 78, those who are healthy will stabilize at that age.[16] Indeed, our patients who have low stress levels and are optimally healthy even in their 70's and 80's have DHEA blood levels higher than many 30-year-olds with unhealthy and highly stressful lifestyles.

DHEA is found in the brain in concentrations equal to those in the adrenal cortex. For many years the role of DHEA was considered to be only an intermediary in sex steroid synthesis but more recently DHEA has been found to prevent cancer and to show strong anti-diabetes effects. There is growing interest in DHEA's role in the treatment of atherosclerosis, hypertension, memory disorders, fat mobilization, cancer prevention, resistance to viral bacteria infections, chronic fatigue, high blood cholesterol, Alzheimer's disease and multiple sclerosis. DHEA acts as a precursor steroid or buffer hormone that alters homeostasis by interacting with many other hormones.

The most recent finding that DHEA has major antioxidant properties is relevant to the entire concept of aging and degenerative disease, as free radicals and lack of antioxidants are increasingly recognized as major correlates with disease, aging and death.[17] The most important metabolic effects of DHEA are:

- Glucose stabilizer
- Regulates all other hormones
- Decreases cholesterol

- Precursor of estrogen and testosterone
- Assists homeostasis after stress reaction
- Enhances immune function
- Maintains youth and health
- Stabilizes weight

STRESS AND THE FOCUS OF ILLNESS

Ultimately all illness is the end result of excess or cumulative stress. Even a fractured bone in a young person is the result of excess direct physical stress. The type of illness, or organ of illness, is most likely the result of genetic predisposition, plus psychological/emotional influences on certain parts of the body. For instance, I have called heart attack or myocardial infarction the popular way to die. Perhaps this disease is the result of distress over inadequate love.

Everyone knows the heart is the energy center for love. Lack of forgiveness, intolerance or the ongoing grief ("broken heart") of a failed love relationship create breakdown of the heart. On the other hand, if the genetic predisposition happened to be in the immune system, the same love loss might result in breast cancer; if one's emotional unfinished business involved insecurity about sexuality, the problem might locate in the sexual organs. As with all aspects of the stress reaction, many factors are involved.

Conventional medicine classifies illnesses as:

- Hereditary or genetic
- Congenital (developed in the 9 months of gestation)
- Traumatic (due to accidents)
- Neoplastic (tumors)
- Infections (bacteria, fungi, viruses)
- Toxic
- Biochemical

- Inflammatory
- Degenerative
- Autoimmune

But none of these classifications explains the underlying cause. Even genetic defects may be "caused" by chemotherapy or X-radiation. In point of fact, the cause of each illness is the total cumulative stress which weakens the body in one or more systems.

Metaphysically, illnesses of the legs may be related to the cumulative stress of one's family ties and sense of safety. Low back and sexual problems always include issues of security and/or sexual hang-ups. Diseases of the upper abdomen relate to our "gut reaction" area, where we carry problems of excess responsibility. Illnesses of the throat, neck and arms include problems of will and communication of needs and desires. Diseases of the brain include problems with use of intuition and wisdom. These more subtle psychosocial issues interact with total chemical, physical, electromagnetic and additional emotional stressors to overwork our adrenals and deplete us of DHEA. As we have seen, DHEA depletion results from excess stress of all types. Then heredity and one's emotional profile determine the site and type of illness.

DHEA MEASUREMENT AND THERAPY

I strongly recommend that any person who has a significant illness at any age, have a DHEA level drawn. In addition, it seems appropriate that all individuals by age 40 should have a baseline DHEA level and if their DHEA is below the optimal, they should begin techniques for restoring DHEA reserves and function. Optimal levels are 750-1250 ng/dL for men and 550-980 ng/dL for women. If your physician will not order this test for you, find a physician who will.

Check the Alternative Medicine Yellow Pages, Future Medicine Publishing, Inc., 5009 Pacific Highway East #6, Fife, WA 98424 or the American Holistic Medical Association, 4101 Lake Boone Trail, Suite 201, Raleigh, NC 27607.

DHEA is quite easily measured with a simple blood test. However, the only laboratory in the country which I have found to be unequivocally reliable is the Corning Nichols Institute, 33608 Ortega Highway, San Juan Capistrano, California 92676, (800) 553-5445. I tried five other laboratories where I sent three separate specimens of exactly the same blood labeled as if they had been taken from three different patients. At those other reference labs, results varied by 50 to 100 percent. At Nichols Lab the variation was 5 percent. I do not recommend getting a DHEA test at any other reference lab as of this writing.

DHEA AND DHEA SULFATE

The total DHEA in the blood stream is a combination of "free" DHEA and DHEA sulfate (DHEA-S), that is a DHEA molecule which has a sulphur molecule attached to it. Although most researchers do not distinguish between DHEA and DHEA-S in either clinical laboratory significance or even in oral replacement therapy, there is some evidence that DHEA-S is not as effective or reliable as DHEA itself.[18-20] It is generally believed that DHEA-S serves as a reservoir of weakly bound DHEA; but there is no clear-cut proof that DHEA-S is fully metabolically available.

This is similar to testosterone. In men, for instance, there is a total testosterone level but a majority of the total testosterone is bound to protein molecules and not available for hormonal use. Only the free testosterone is actually a reflection of testosterone activity. The same may well be true for DHEA.

For instance, in 108 HIV seropositive men with low levels of the critical CD4 lymphocytes, DHEA levels were predictive of progression to AIDS but DHEA-S levels were not. With ACTH administration, DHEA increased only slightly in elderly subjects with significantly less increase in DHEA-S.

With administration of corticotropin releasing factor, DHEA levels increased 60 percent in both young and old individuals. The DHEA sulfate did not increase. Thus, my recommendation is to stick with DHEA itself as both a measurement and as a replacement, if DHEA is to be used.

ORAL DHEA THERAPY

DHEA replacement therapy has been reported to be successful in a wide variety of illnesses. An increased sense of well-being and improved memory have been commonly reported. Improved insulin sensitivity and improved control of diabetes have also been reported.[18] DHEA has been found to assist in weight loss but only in significantly obese individuals. In fact, patents have been issued for all the following uses of DHEA:

- Reducing body fat mass while increasing muscle mass.
- Lowering HDL cholesterol and preventing atherosclerosis.
- Lowering platelet aggregation to reduce the incidence of myocardial infarction and stroke.
- Reducing the symptoms of prostatic hypertrophy as well as the symptoms of menopause and decreased libido.
- Treating rheumatoid arthritis, psoriasis, lupus and other autoimmune diseases.
- Treating diabetes.

DHEA was regulated by the FDA and categorized in the same group with codeine until 1996. It is now available in most drug and health food stores. However, it is unwise to self-prescribe this powerful hormone. There is no need to take it unless you are deficient or have a serious illness and a level in the poor range. A test of DHEA blood levels and supervision by a health professional are strongly recommended.

There are some illnesses in which the steroid drugs cortisone or prednisone are essential to maintain life or function. Perhaps the most crucial is brain or spinal cord swelling or in certain acute infections which cause toxic shock. Temporal arteritis, a severe autoimmune inflammatory disorder affecting the arteries of the brain, is another. In all these situations, when steroids are needed, the complications of excess cortisone-like drugs could be largely prevented if large doses of DHEA were administered concomitantly. Indeed, I believe DHEA supplementation is essential for anyone on long-term steroids for optimal benefit. The one exception might be in patients with organ transplants where steroids are used to suppress the immune system's rejection tendencies. Further research should be done in this field. In every other situation where steroids are administered, DHEA should be added as well.

DHEA oral supplementation has been used at doses up to 4,000 mg per day. At large doses of DHEA, testosterone, estrogen and androstenediol all increase.

In multiple sclerosis, dosages of DHEA up to 4,000 mg per day appear to lead to significant improvement in patients, with decreased numbness and spasticity.

Finally in aging men and women, administration of just 100 mg/day of DHEA has led to remarkable increase in both physical and psychological well-being. Muscle mass and muscle strength improved, as did immune function, especially natural killer cell function.[19]

When to use DHEA Supplementation

If your DHEA blood level is less than 180 ng/dL in a woman or 220 ng/dL in a man and if you have any serious illness (heart disease, rheumatoid arthritis, lupus, multiple sclerosis, a serious infection, need for a major operation, etc.) then you should be placed on oral DHEA in dosages adequate to bring your blood levels up to at least 400 to 450 ng/dL in a woman or 600 to 650 ng/dL in a man.

Individual dosages may range from 25 mg twice a day to 250 mg four times a day. Only repeated blood tests will determine the best dosage.

At the same time, you should be started on a DHEA restoration program. After three to four months, oral DHEA supplementation should be withdrawn over a two to four week period, while continuing stimulation (see page 29). One week after DHEA is stopped, recheck the blood level of DHEA and if you are now above 180 ng/dL in a woman or 220 ng/dL in a man, continue on the restoration program.

NATURAL TECHNIQUES FOR ENHANCING DHEA PRODUCTION

Natural enhancement of DHEA has been reported with physical exercise[20], stress reduction programs and transcendental meditation[21], as well as caloric restriction.[22] It is of some interest that DHEA enhances the hypnotic and hypothermic effects of both ethanol and pentobarbital.[23] In 10 to 16-year-old athletes, DHEA is significantly higher than in non-athletes. Pubic hair, testosterone, testicular volume and bone age are also greater in athletes, as is growth hormone and cortisol. Adrenal hyperactivity is actually proposed as the "cause" of this difference in athletes; but it appears to be, at least at that age, a healthy hyperactivity. On the other hand, the Circadian rhythm of DHEA, progesterone and cortisol is extinguished during prolonged physical stress with deficiencies in sleep.[24] As in everything else, moderation is the key.

Serum DHEA is higher in all age groups of women and most age groups of men who practice transcendental meditation regularly. DHEA levels in meditators are comparable to those of non-meditators five to 10 years younger.

RECENT INNOVATIONS IN DHEA RESTORATION

Although higher levels of DHEA have been reported with those who exercise regularly and meditate regularly, these approaches have not been tested as specific treatment of DHEA or adrenoandrogen deficiency.

Having found DHEA deficiency to be remarkably common in patients with depression and chronic fatigue syndrome, we began in 1991 to explore techniques which might assist the body in recovering its ability to produce DHEA naturally and safely. Although the standard literature did not suggest a relation between progesterone and DHEA, we theorized that it might be possible to convert progesterone into DHEA. This theory proved profitable.

Over the last four years, we have demonstrated at the Shealy Institute that three percent natural progesterone cream raises DHEA levels 40 to 100 percent in most individuals, both men and women. Natural progesterone will be discussed more fully on page 33.

With that successful beginning, we began exploring other possible techniques for enhancing DHEA production. Acupuncture has been reported to alleviate pre-menstrual syndrome as well as restitution of fertility in men. The acupuncture circuit used for regulation of gonadal (ovarian or testicular) function also has additional points for adrenal and thyroid regulation but none for the pituitary. I selected additional acupuncture points for the pituitary and brain-body connection. We then proceeded to apply two types of electrical stimulation to these 12 acupuncture points.

The first stimulator, GigaTENS™, has been widely used in the Ukraine, applied to acupuncture points, to treat a variety of problems. According to Ukrainian quantum physicists, GigaTENS is more powerful than one microvolt of energy at frequencies of 52 to 78 billion cycles per second. Giga-TENS was applied daily to the 12 points of the Ring of Fire (see Chart 5), three minutes per point for 10 days and then once a week for 10 additional weeks.

The results were most gratifying. Average blood levels of DHEA went up 56 percent. Equally important, in 21 patients with diabetic neuropathy, a painful deterioration of nerves, 17 patients reported marked reduction in pain, as well as improved sensation and decreased insulin requirements. No other known treatment can arrest or reverse diabetic polyneuropathy.

And in 50 patients with painful rheumatoid arthritis, which had not responded to cortisone-like drugs, 35 had substantial reduction in pain. Thus, GigaTENS stimulation of the Ring of Fire appears to be the most successful treat-

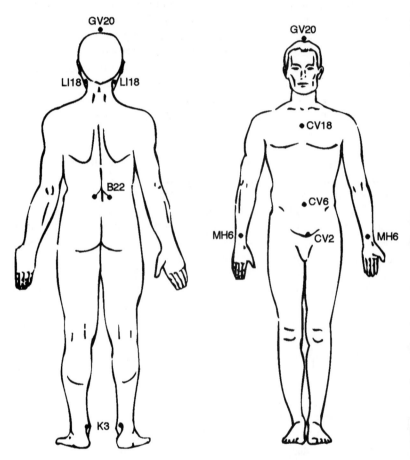

CHART 5. The Ring of Fire Points

ment to date for these two crippling diseases. At least part of the effect is the result of DHEA enhancement.

Since GigaTENS it not yet available for widespread use, we then turned to another stimulator, the Liss cranial electrical stimulator, which has been used for over 20 years to treat pain. In over 9,000 patients, we've found considerable benefit with the Liss cranial electrical stimulator. Fifty percent of chronically depressed patients improved with daily cranial electrical stimulation within two weeks with no undesirable side effects and no drugs. The Liss cranial electrical stimulator has been found to raise both serotonin and beta-endorphin levels, helping restore those two essential neurochemicals in hundreds of chronically depressed patients.

But when we applied the Liss cranial electrical stimulator transcranially in 50 depressed patients, DHEA levels did not improve even when the depression lifted.

We then tried the Liss cranial electrical stimulator on the 12 Ring of Fire points, five minutes per point, using the stimulator on two points at a time, so that the entire treatment takes only 30 minutes. This application has resulted in average increases of 63 percent in DHEA levels; ranges of increase have been 40 percent to over 100 percent.

Finally, we have combined these three approaches using progesterone plus the Liss cranial electrical stimulator or GigaTENS; or using all three at the same time. In combination, these treatments lead to DHEA increases of up to 300 percent; average increases are over 93 percent.

The Ring of Fire consists of the following points:

- Bilateral Kidney (K3)
- Conception Vessel (CV 1 or 2)
- Conception Vessel (CV 6)
- Bilateral Bladder (B 22)
- Conception Vessel (CV 18)
- Bilateral Master of the Heart (MH 6)
- Bilateral Large Intestine (LI 18)
- Governing Vessel (GV 20)

In individuals who are quite ill, we prefer to give DHEA supplements to bring up the blood level to an optimal level and to keep them at that level for several months while stimulating them with progesterone cream and at least the Liss stimulator or GigaTENS on the Ring of Fire points.

Two case histories are worth mentioning. A 58-year-old woman presented to us with severe angina at the beginning of a mild heart attack. Her blood DHEA level was only 47 ng/dL. She was treated appropriately for the heart attack but at the same time, we placed her on DHEA, initially 400 mg a day and gradually reduced that to 100 mg a day. At the same time, she was placed on progesterone cream and application of the Liss stimulator to the Ring of Fire points. Four months later she was withdrawn from the oral DHEA, continued on stimulation, and given one shot of ACTH (adrenocorticotropin hormone) and one of Factrel (luteinizing releasing factor). Following that, her DHEA level was 381 ng/dL, not optimal but certainly well above the serious deficiency level with which we started. Her energy and well-being were the greatest they had been in years.

In a 78-year-old woman with severe diabetic neuropathy, the initial DHEA was only 87 ng/dL, well below normal. She had total paralysis of both feet, as well as intractable pain. In her case, GigaTENS activation of the Ring of Fire led to 90 percent reduction in pain, considerable improvement in normal sensation and adequate strength in the right foot to be able to walk without her foot-drop brace. Her DHEA came up to 210 ng/dL.

The technology described in this section is so unique and critically important that I have applied for a patent on the various components: application of progesterone cream and application of CES or GigaTENS to the Ring of Fire points.

Your Take-home Message

A majority of Americans have a lifestyle which is more stressful than desirable. Chronic stress depletes them of DHEA reserves and eventually leads to illness. If you are over age 30 or have significant illness, first find a physician willing to work with you in assessing your blood DHEA level. If your level is below 550 ng/dL for women or below 750 ng/dL for men, begin at once to apply 3 percent natural progesterone cream and use the Liss cranial electrical stimulator on the Ring of Fire points. If you have a significant illness and DHEA is less than 130 ng/dL in women or less than 180 ng/dL in men, then you should be treated with DHEA supplements adequate to raise blood levels to the optimal ones listed above. At the same time, begin progesterone cream and the Liss cranial electrical stimulator on the Ring of Fire points. After three to six months, wean from oral DHEA, continue the stimulation and recheck DHEA levels to be sure you have been jump started!

NATURAL PROGESTERONE

Dr. John Lee has done more work on the use of natural progesterone than any other researcher.[25] Natural progesterone is produced primarily from wild yams (dioscorea). As such, it is quite inexpensive and cannot be patented. Thus, in order to manufacture a synthetic patentable progesterone derivative, pharmaceutical companies made a number of changes in progesterone, giving it a somewhat more prolonged activity, but with many unwelcome side effects. These pharmaceutical drugs (such as Provera) are called progestins, progestogens and gestagens. They are synthetic, not natural progesterone. As such, they do not provide the full spectrum of natural progesterone's biological activity and not one of them is totally safe.

Fortunately, natural progesterone is easily absorbed through the skin. As a precursor of both estrogen and testosterone, natural progesterone has many benefits:

- It prevents fibrocystic disease of the breasts.
- It is a natural diuretic.
- It helps in the metabolic burning of fat for energy.
- It is a natural antidepressant.
- It helps in regulating thyroid hormone activity.
- It assists in normal blood clotting.
- It enhances libido.
- It helps stabilize blood sugar levels.
- It protects against cancer of the uterus and the breasts.

- It helps prevent osteoporosis.
- It is essential for production of cortisone in the adrenal cortex.

An imbalance of progesterone with a relative estrogen predominance can result in premenstrual symptoms such as water retention, edema, breast swelling and mood swings. Thus natural progesterone can be helpful in treating PMS as well as in raising DHEA levels.

Perhaps the most important benefit of natural progesterone supplementation, however, is in the prevention and treatment of osteoporosis. Dr. Lee has demonstrated that natural progesterone cream used at a dose of approximately ¼ teaspoon twice a day applied to skin, coupled with adequate aerobic exercise, 800 to 1000 mg calcium, 300 mg magnesium, 15 to 30 mg zinc, 15 mg beta carotene, 2000 mg vitamin C, 400 units vitamin D, avoiding smoking, and minimizing alcohol and red meat leads to better treatment and prevention of osteoporosis than any other known approach.

I believe that natural progesterone cream derived from wild yam extract should be used by almost every mature adult, female or male, especially those who have DHEA blood levels below optimal. The most common cause of death in elderly women is from the complications of fracture of the hip from osteoporosis. Such fractures are also remarkably common in men. I believe that progesterone cream could do more to preserve health and well-being in elderly people than all the drugs in the world. A natural progesterone cream such as Pro-Gest Cream can be purchased in most health food stores.

When selecting a 3-percent natural progesterone cream, it is important not to select one labeled simply "diosgenin" or "diosorea." I have been besieged with mailings about these products, which claim to be natural precursors for DHEA. However, I tried one of these supplements on three patients and over a period of two months, there was no increase in their DHEA. In two other individuals, a different mail-order product called "extract of wild yam," also did not raise their very low DHEA levels. At this time, I cannot recommend simple diosgenin or wild yam for raising DHEA. Nor are there any other herbs known to raise DHEA at this writing. The progesterone creams such as Progest cream that seem to work are *synthesized* from diosgenin or wild yam and thus are more potent.

In one of the most significant studies on progesterone, physicians at Johns Hopkins University in 1981 reported on the incidence of breast cancer in 1083 women who had been followed for 13 to 33 years. In this group of women, those who had endogenous progesterone deficiency were 5.4 times as likely to develop breast cancer as premenopausal women who did not have endogenous progesterone deficiency. This was an extremely well done study and there was no difference between the two groups of women in ages of menarche or menopause, history of oral contraceptive use, history of benign breast disease or age at the first pregnancy. Women with progesterone deficiency had a ten-fold increase in deaths from all malignant neoplasms compared with those who did not have progesterone deficiency. It is interesting to speculate that those women who were deficient in progesterone almost certainly were deficient in DHEA as well. Natural progesterone replacement theoretically could have improved their health and probably prevented this much higher incidence of cancer in general and breast cancer in particular. This is another striking bit of evidence that progesterone is a critically important hormone. There is no evidence natural progesterone has any harmful side effects.[26]

Men are totally ignored in the medical literature as far as progesterone is concerned. Men have blood levels of progesterone throughout life similar to levels in women after age 45 or 50. While women experience menopause, men experience andropause with declining levels of testosterone and all the associated degenerative processes, most particularly osteoporosis. While usually not as severe as the osteoporosis in women, it is still a major disease of aging. As we have demonstrated, progesterone applied to men leads to increased DHEA levels and improved libido. Every male with DHEA levels below 600 ng/dL should use natural progesterone cream, except men with prostate cancer. At this time, I would recommend that men with prostate cancer stimulate the Ring of Fire to enhance DHEA.

DHEA DEFICIENCY IN VARIOUS DISEASES

Many authors have reported low levels of DHEA in diabetes,[27] coronary artery disease,[28,29] various cancers,[30,31] obesity,[32] lupus erythematosus, hypertension,[33] AIDS,[34,35] viral infections, Alzheimer's disease, and multiple sclerosis. DHEA appears to be a major modulator of the stress reaction in relation to the increase of glucocorticoid or cortisol[36] and in animals, at least, it is felt to be anxiolytic (reduces anxiety).[37] The DHEA deficiency is a reflection of the maladaptation in all these stress illnesses.

It is interesting to note that increased testosterone and DHEA are associated with lower insulin levels in men but in women increased levels of testosterone and DHEA are associated with hyperinsulinemia and insulin resistance.[38]

DHEA is decreased when individuals are given dexamethasone and almost certainly all other forms of cortisol and prednisone.

In a group of older men and women from 77 to 79 years of age, the higher functioning subjects all had higher levels of DHEA and many fewer psychiatric symptoms.[39]

Increased amounts of total fat on the trunk and decreased amounts of total fat on the legs are associated with increased blood levels of DHEA in normally menstruating females. So if you have fat legs, check your DHEA levels!

DHEA prevents dexamethasone-induced hypertension in rats.

In post-menopausal patients with advanced breast cancer, DHEA is progressively decreased.

Although DHEA circulates in a circadian rhythm it is far less significant than in many other hormones. Normal changes from morning to afternoon or evening or even from season to season do not exceed about 15 percent, whereas with cortisol levels, ranges from morning to evening vary by up to 100 percent.

DHEA blocks the normal increase in tryptophan hydroxylase, a precursor of serotonin, antagonizing the effects of glucocorticoids. This is a steroid specific event with no similar effect from estrogen, androgen or progesterone.

DHEA modulates diabetes, obesity, carcinogenesis, tumor growth, stress, pregnancy, hypertension, collagen and skin integrity, fatigue, depression, memory and immune responses. A major effect of DHEA is on the inhibition of glucose 6 phosphate dehydrogenase, which explains its major role in diabetes.

DIABETES

DHEA's major role under normal circumstances is as a homeostatic mechanism in the basic stress reaction. When one is stressed, cortisol is released to raise blood sugar levels. This is followed by the release of glycogen from the liver, which is broken down into glucose and released into the bloodstream. This in turn releases insulin to burn the extra glucose. Thus, gradual maladaptation in the glucose-insulin regulatory mechanism may be the first stage for decreases in DHEA. The antiviral and other benefits of DHEA are probably indirectly due to the normal modulation of the homeostatic insulin-glucose effects.

Caffeine, nicotine and sugar are dangerous because all of them induce a stress reaction and raise blood sugar levels. This results in an eventual maladaptation and the inability of the body to manufacture adequate DHEA to regulate the system. Thus hypoglycemia, the earliest stage of maladaptation of glucose-insulin regulation, and hyperglycemia, when the pancreas has been essentially burned out and can no longer make insulin, are both reflections of the earliest stages of maladaptation. In general, except in the acute onset of juvenile diabetes (which may be the result of viral damage to the pancreas) it is likely that most diabetic individuals go through a hypoglycemic stage first with an excess of insulin produced, resulting in the symptoms of nervousness, anxiety, sweating, hunger and various mood changes. Insufficient insulin and the high blood sugar of diabetes develop later.

Diabetes, of course, is one of the major causes of death in the United States and diabetes is associated with a marked increase in the incidence of high blood pressure, heart disease and stroke.

Early in the course of diabetes, there is a loss of sensitivity to insulin. In mice at least, DHEA increases sensitivity to insulin and early treatment of these pre-diabetic mice prevented many of the symptoms of diabetes. DHEA administration reduced blood sugar concentrations to normal.[40,41]

DHEA is almost certainly the treatment of choice in the early stages of diabetes, especially Type 2 or adult onset diabetes. Anyone who has a diagnosis of diabetes should obviously take all of the standard steps that are useful in treating diabetes such as reducing total calories, increasing exercise and decreasing stress with deep relaxation techniques. But the most essential treatment should be a measurement of DHEA levels. If the DHEA blood level is below 550 ng/dL in a woman or below 750 ng/dL in a man, then either natural stimulation of the body to raise DHEA or supplementation with DHEA should be considered. I believe it is far safer than any of the antidiabetic drugs, including insulin.

ATHEROSCLEROSIS, HEART DISEASE AND STROKE

Coronary artery disease and stroke kill far more people than cancer. The relationship of low DHEA with coronary artery disease and the lower incidence of heart disease in people with higher levels of DHEA are among the most striking findings. As noted earlier, there have been numerous studies that show these relationships. Since DHEA regulates fat metabolism and higher levels of DHEA are associated with far less atherosclerosis, it is obvious that DHEA has many more important benefits in helping to prevent cardiovascular disease. If everyone by age 40 had a DHEA level drawn and began rejuvenation of the DHEA system, I believe we would see a marked decrease in the risk of cardiovascular disease. On the other hand, in those individuals who have already had a stroke or coronary occlusion, it is even more imperative that DHEA levels be raised to optimal (550 ng/dL or above in women and 750 ng/dL or above in men). In addition, it is my strong recommendation that any individual who is having a coronary artery occlusion or a heart attack should immediately be placed on large doses of DHEA, probably 500 mg of DHEA twice a day for at least the next three months. At that point, they should be weaned from the DHEA while having their blood level monitored. Within a month after the coronary occlusion, I believe they should start on rejuvenation of the body's ability to make its own DHEA (see Natural Techniques for Enhancing DHEA Production, page 28). After three to four months, they should be weaned from the DHEA supplementation to determine whether they have recovered sufficient natural ability to make DHEA so they no longer need oral DHEA supplementation.

MENOPAUSE/ANDROPAUSE

In patients between 50 and 79 years of age, DHEA levels are 40 percent lower in women and 35 percent lower in men who have cardiovascular disease than in those without cardiovascular disease. These results may be due to menopause or andropause. No other sex hormone (estrone, estradiol, testosterone or androstenedione) showed such decreases after age 50. It is particularly important to note that women on hormone replacement therapy (HRT) had *lower* DHEA levels than those not on HRT. Premarin and other estrogen replacements do not raise DHEA levels and carry many risks. Natural progesterone, on the other hand, can actually increase bone density, carries no known risks and elevates DHEA.

It appears that both men and women become relatively deficient in progesterone after age 50. This deficiency may be aggravated by smoking as well as obesity. Body fat produces estrogen, even in men, leading to excess estrogen and lowered progesterone. This decrease in progesterone is almost certainly partially responsible for the declining DHEA levels often reported with aging. Excess and cumulative stress additionally lowers DHEA, weakening the immune system.

Both syndromes of menopause and andropause (lowered testosterone production in men) as well as the many diseases increasing after age 50 may be prevented with appropriate, safe therapies. You can begin with exercise.

It is never too late to start an exercise program. Walk at a comfortable pace for five minutes daily, after one week add one or two minutes. Increase weekly until you reach 60 minutes at least six days per week. Then increase your pace so that eventually you can comfortably walk four miles in 60 minutes.

Alternatively, get a mini-trampoline. Don't jog. Just stand in place, feet flat and walk in place, just bending your knees alternately. Start with two to three minutes and build slowly. Once you reach 60 minutes of walking or gentle trampolining, you may explore other exercise.

Be sure to spend at least one hour per day outside. You don't have to be in the sun, but in natural light.

Next, eat a diet relatively low in fat and very low in sugar; minimize caffeine. Eat fish three to four times per week, chicken or turkey one to three times, and beef not more than once per week.

Don't smoke. Minimize alcohol. Meditate at least 30 minutes per day. Keep a positive attitude.

Finally, find a doctor who will check your DHEA. If it is below optimal, add natural progesterone cream, ¼ teaspoon on the skin, twice a day. If DHEA does not come up enough, increase to ¼ teaspoon four times a day. And if DHEA is still low, get a prescription for the Liss cranial electrical stimulator and use it on the Ring of Fire points.

With this approach, you should be able to improve your well-being, your overall health and your longevity. I believe that natural life expectancy should be at least 100 years. These healthy lifestyle habits should allow you to realize that potential.

CANCER

The incidence of cancer in America continues to increase each year. No one knows whether this is due to environmental pollutants, the increase in smoking among young women, our high-fat nutrient-poor diet or whether our modern, over-stressed society has depleted DHEA levels, predisposing more and more people to cancer. Every type of cancer which has been studied has been associated with very low levels of DHEA and there is some evidence that giving DHEA can help in cancer remission in some patients. Obviously, as with all disease, the most effort must be put into prevention. If an individual has a baseline DHEA any time after age 30 or 40 which is below the optimal, by far the most important treatment they can undertake is restoration of DHEA levels to the optimal (see Natural Techniques for Enhancing DHEA Production, page 28).

As with diabetes and cardiovascular disease, we recommend all individuals strive for an optimal level of DHEA; first as a natural health enhancer and secondly for assistance in treating major diseases. In patients who have cancer, I recommend large doses of DHEA while monitoring the disease. Once cancer remission is unequivocal, then the dosage of DHEA might be reduced over a three to four month period while DHEA restoration is being attempted.

In women with breast cancer or uterine or ovarian cancer and in men with prostate cancer, I would not recommend the use of natural progesterone cream even though there is no evidence at this time that it would be harmful. From the theoretical point of view, I would not use progesterone in these individuals, because progesterone has a stronger effect in raising testosterone and estrogen than does DHEA. On the other hand, I certainly think that oral DHEA replacement is valid in all such situations.

AUTOIMMUNE DISEASES

Among the most common diseases affecting the human race are the autoimmune diseases which include rheumatoid arthritis, lupus erythematosus, scleroderma, most cases of polyneuropathy, amyotrophic lateral sclerosis and multiple sclerosis. In all of these diseases, DHEA supplementation is worth serious consideration. There is good evidence that lupus can be more satisfactorily treated with DHEA than with Prednisone without any of the side effects from corti-sone/prednisone administration. Even in patients who are on Prednisone, I believe that DHEA supplementation is worth consideration while they are in the process of being weaned from this medication. Consider this case history:

Holly G. is a 50-year-old woman with lupus erythemato-sus who has been on 20 mg of Prednisone daily for three years with very minimal effect upon her major symptom which is polyarthralgia or arthritis. Her DHEA level was less than 100 ng/dL. We placed her on just 200 mg of DHEA orally per day and over a period of six weeks, weaned her off Prednisone. All of her arthralgia symptoms were totally controlled and she felt the best she had in years.

OBESITY

Obesity is perhaps the most controversial illness for which DHEA supplementation may be indicated. Yet, there is no doubt that DHEA serves to enhance fat metabolism and to assist in weight reduction in patients who are overweight. In a research study, dogs placed on a high fiber diet lost 31 percent of their body weight, whereas those placed on a high fiber diet plus DHEA lost 65.7 percent of their excess body weight.[42] Even without the high fiber diet, 68 percent of the dogs experienced weight loss of four percent per month with just DHEA supplementation.[43] In obese men, there was a 31 percent decrease in body fat in the men treated with DHEA (exactly the same as in dogs!).[44] Interestingly, there was no change in body weight; however a 31 percent decrease in body fat is quite significant. In rats at least, DHEA supplementation leads to a voluntary reduction in food intake.[45] Apparently DHEA curbs hunger. It is well known that estrogen can be produced in fat tissue and in obese men there is a decrease in both testosterone and DHEA levels and an increase in estrogen. Certainly in patients who are significantly obese, DHEA supplementation should be considered along with the usual increased physical exercise and decreased caloric intake, as well as some effort at stress reduction through daily deep relaxation.

The latest research on DHEA in obesity reveals that weight loss leads to insulin reduction and a 125 percent increase in DHEA in men.[46]

DEPRESSION

My own findings of low DHEA in patients with depression have most recently been reinforced by a report that DHEA is both an antidepressant and cognition enhancer in patients with major depression. Dosages as low as 30 to 90 mg per day were beneficial.[47] We have never seen a depressed patient with optimal levels of DHEA. And no one we've seen with optimal levels of DHEA is depressed. An interesting corollary is that there are only three significant illnesses in which DHEA levels are higher than average: schizophrenia, extreme agitation and alcoholism. None of these is recommended to raise your DHEA! Extreme agitation is found not only in people with panic attacks but those chronically and perpetually agitated on the verge of an emotional breakdown. At that point, DHEA is exhausted.

Alcoholism is more difficult to explain. Alcohol acts much like sugar, leading to insulin release and potential DHEA depletion. Alcoholics appear to go through at least two major stages; that of chronic alcoholism which allows them to drown their sorrows in alcohol, avoiding the emotional anxiety they might otherwise experience. For some time, this may allow them to maintain normal levels of DHEA. Sooner or later, however, exhaustion occurs and the diseases of alcoholism, such as cirrhosis or brain and nerve damage, manifest. At that point, DHEA is depleted.

CONTRAINDICATIONS TO DHEA SUPPLEMENTATION

There are no reported significant complications of DHEA supplementation. Minimal acne has been reported and, rarely, mild facial hair growth in older women, but older women often have significant facial hair growth anyway.

I do not recommend DHEA supplementation or the use of progesterone cream in women with cancer of the breast, ovary or uterus or men with cancer of the prostate, because those are hormonally influenced cancers.

On the other hand, I quite routinely use the electrical stimulation of the Ring of Fire with either the GigaTENS or the Liss cranial electrical stimulator in these individuals. We are most hopeful that within a year we will have available an outstanding electrical stimulator that can be sold over-the-counter without the need for a prescription.

CONCLUSION

Burn-out is the current popular term for exhaustion and exhaustion is the end result of stress. DHEA is depleted by chronic stress and anything which reduces stress or increases DHEA is good for you, assisting in maintaining health throughout a long and productive life.

The best way to maintain health through a long life is to live a healthy lifestyle:

- Eat a healthy diet.
- Avoid nicotine and junk food.
- Minimize caffeine, alcohol and sugar.
- Exercise regularly.
- Spend time outside daily.
- Avoid excessive air or automobile travel.
- Practice deep relaxation or meditation daily.
- Resolve your anger, guilt, anxiety or depression.

Check your blood level of DHEA and if yours is below the optimal level (750 ng/dL or above in men, 550 ng/dL or above in women), being a restoration program. You are worth the time and effort.

REFERENCES

1. Hans Selye, *Stress Without Distress*, (Philadelphia: J. B. Lippincott, Co., 1974).
2. C. Norman Shealy. 1984. "Total Life Stress and Symptomatology," *Journal of Holistic Medicine*, 6(2):112–129.
3. V. M. Dilman and W. Dean, 1992. "The Neuroendocrine Theory of Aging and Degenerative Disease," The Center for Bio-Gerontology, Pensacola, pp. 43–62.
4. M. Kalimi and W. Regelson (editors), *The Biologic Role of Dehydroepiandrosterone (DHEA)*, (Berlin, New York: Walter de Gruyter, 1990), pp. 331–360.
5. M.D. Majewska, "Neuronal Actions of DHEAS: Implications for Aging," Dehydroepiandrosterone (DHEA) and Aging, New York Academy of Sciences Meeting, June 17–19, 1995.
6. E. Berton, D. Hoover, H. Fein, R. Galloway and R. Smallridge, "Adaptation to Chronic Stress in Military Trainees: Adrenal Androgens, Testosterone, Glucocorticoids, IGF-1 and Immune Function," Dehydroepiandrosterone (DHEA) and Aging, New York Academy of Sciences Meeting, June 17–19, 1995.
7. B. Araneo, "Proof-of-Principle Studies Illustrating the Unique Adjuvant Effects of DHEAS in the Immunization of Elderly Humans," Dehydroepiandrosterone (DHEA) and Aging, New York Academy of Sciences Meeting, June 17–19, 1995.

8. C. N. Falany and K. A. Comer, "Human DHEA Sulfotransferase: Purification Molecular Cloning and Characterization," Dehydroepiandrosterone (DHEA) and Aging, New York Academy of Sciences Meeting, June 17–19, 1995.

9. W. Regelson and W. Pierpaoli. 1987. "Melatonin: A Rediscovered Antitumor Hormone? Its Relation to Surface Receptors; Sex Steroid Metabolism, Immunologic Response and Chronobiologic Factors in Tumor Growth and Therapy," Cancer Investigation 5(4):379–385.

10. J. E. Nestler, N.A. Beer, D. J. Jakubowicz, and R.M. Beer. 1994. "Effects of a Reduction in Circulating Insulin by Metformin on Serum Dehydroepiandrosterone Sulfate in Nondiabetic Men," Clin. Endocrinol. Metab. 78(3):549–554.

11. J. E. Nestler, "Regulation of Human DHEA Metabolism by Insulin," Dehydroepiandrosterone (DHEA) and Aging, New York Academy of Sciences Meeting, June 17–19, 1995.

12. A. B. Littman, M. Fava, P. Halperin, S. Lamon-Fava, F.R. Drews, M.A. Oleshansky, C. C. Bielenda, and R.A. MacLaughlin. 1993. "Physiologic Benefits of a Stress Reduction Program for Healthy Middle-Aged Army Officers," J. Psychosom. Res. 37(4):345–354.

13. R. J. Ruiz Salmeron, J. L. del Arbol, J. Torrededia, J. Raya Munoz, A. Lopez Luque, J. Rico Irles, and J. Golanos. 1992. "Dehidroepiandrosterona-Sulfato y Lipidos en el Infargo Agudo de Miocardio," Rev. Clin Esp. 190(8):398–402.

14. F. Stahl, D. Schnorr, C. Pilz, and G. Dorner. 1992. "Dehydroepiandrosterone Levels in Patients with Prostatic Cancer, Heart Disease and Under Surgery Stress," Exp. Clin. Endocrinol. 99(2):68–70.

15. M. Namiki. 1994. "Aged People and Stress," Nippon Ronen Igakkai Zasshi 31(2):85–95.

16. W. Eggert-Kruse, W. Kruse, G. Rohr, S. Muller, D. Kreissler-Haag, K. Klinga, and B. Runnebaum. 1994. "Hormone Profile of Elderly Women and Potential Modifiers," Geburtshilfe Frauenheilkd, 54(6):321–331.

17. P. K. Siiteri, D. Draves, D. Fraser and D. Stites, "Antioxidant Properties of DHEAS, Dehydroepiandrosterone (DHEA) and Aging, New York Academy of Sciences Meeting, June 17–19, 1995.

18. C.K. Buffington, G. Pourmotabbed, and A. E. Kitabchi. 1993. "Case Report: Amelioration of Insulin Resistance in Diabetes with Dehydroepiandrosterone," Am. J. Med. Sci. 306(5):320–324.

19. S. Lieberman, "An Abbreviated Account of Some Aspects of the Biochemistry of DHEA," Dehydroepiandrosterone (DHEA) and Aging, New York Academy of Sciences Meeting, June 17–19, 1995.

20. E. Cacciari, L. Mazzanti, D. Tassinari, R. Bergamaschi, C. Magnani, F. Zappulla, G. Nanni, C. Cobianchi, T. Ghini, R. Pini, G. Tani. 1990. "Effects of Sport (Football) on Growth: Auxological, Anthropometric and Hormonal Aspects," Eur. J. Appl. Physiol. 61:149–158.

21. J.L. Glaser, J. L. Brind, J. H. Vogelman, M. J. Eisner, M.C. Dillbeck, R. K. Wallace, D. Chopra, N. Orentreich. 1992. "Elevated Serum Dehydroepiandrosterone Sulfate Levels in Practitioners of the Transcendental Meditation (TM) and TM-Siddhi program," J. Behav. Med. 15(4):327–341.

22. A. Turturro and R. W. Hart. 1991. "Longevity-assurance mechanisms and caloric restriction, Annals New York Academy of Sciences, 621:363–372.

23. C. L. Melchior and R. F. Ritzmann. 1992. "Dehydroepiandrosterone Enhances the Hypnotic and Hypothermic Effects of Ethanol and Pentobarbital," Pharmacol. Biochem. Behav., 43(1):223–227.

24. K. Opstad. 1994. "Circadian Rhythm of Hormones Is Extinguished During Prolonged Physical Stress, Sleep and Energy Deficiency in Young Men," *Eur. J. Endocrinol.* 131(1):56–66.

25. John Lee, *Natural Progesterone: The Multiple Roles of A Remarkable Hormone,* (Sebastopol, Calif.: BLL Publishing) 1993.

26. Linda D. Cowan, Leon Gordis, James Tonascia and Georgeanna Seegar Jones. 1981. "Breast Cancer Incidence in Women with a History of Progesterone Deficiency," *Amer. Jrnl. of Epid.* 114(2):209–217.

27. J. E. Nestler, J. N. Clore, and W. G. Blackard, "Dehydroepiandrosterone: (DHEA) the "missing link" Between Hyperinsulinemia and Atherosclerosis?" *FASEB J.* 6(12):3073–3075.

28. G. B. Gordon, E. D. Bush, and H. F. Weisman. 1988. "Reduction of Atherosclerosis by Administration of Dehydroepiandrosterone (DHEA). A Study in the Hypercholesterolemic New Zealand White Rabbit with Aortic Intimal Injury," *J. Clin. Invest.* 82(2):712–720.

29. E. Barrett-Connor, K.T. Khaw, and S.S. Yen. 1986. "A Prospective Study of Dehydroepiandrosterone (DHEA) Sulfate, Mortality, and Cardiovascular Disease," *New England Journal of Medicine* 315(24):1519–1524.

30. F. Giona, L. Annino, P. Donato and M. Ermini. 1994. "Gonadal, Adrenal, Androgen and Thyroid Functions in Adults Treated for Acute Lymphoblastic Leukemia," *Haematologica* 79(2):141–147.

31. J.M. Bhatavdekar, D.D. Patel, P.R. Chikhlikar, R. H. Mehta, H.H. Vora, N.H. Karelia, N. Ghosh, N.G. Shah, T.P. Suthar, and J.P. Neema. 1994. "Levels of Circulating Peptide and Steroid Hormones in Men with Lung Cancer," *Neoplasma* (41(2):101–103.

32. D.P. Williams, T. W. Boyden, R. W. Pamenter, T.G. Lohman, S.B. Going. 1993. "Relationship of Body Fat Percentage and Fat Distribution with Dehydroepiandrosterone Sulfate in Premenopausal Females," *J. Clin. Endocrinol. Metab.* 77(1):80–85.

33. Y. Shafagoj, J. Opoku, D. Qureshi, W. Regelson and M. Kalimi. 1992. "Dehydroepiandrosterone Prevents Dexamethasone-Induced Hypertension in Rats," *Am. J. Physiol.* 263(2pt 1):E210–213.

34. T.L. Wisniewski, C.W. Hilton, E.V. Morse and F. Svec. 1993. "The Relationship of Serum DHEA-S and Cortisol Levels to Measures of Immune Function in Human Immunodeficiency Virus-Related Illness," *Am. J. Med. Sci.* 305(2):79–83.

35. J. W. Mulder, P.H. Frissen, P. Krijnen, E. Endert, F. de Wolf, J. Goudsmit, J.G. Masterson and J.M. Lange. 1992. "Dehydroepiandrosterone as Predictor for Progression to AIDS in Asymptomatic Human Immunodeficiency Virus-Infected Men, *J. Infect. Dis.,* 165(3):413–418.

36. V.B. Singh, M. Kalimi, T.H. Phan and M.C. Boadle-Biber. 1994. "Intracranial Dehydro-Epiandrosterone Blocks the Activation of Tryptophan Hydroxylase in Response to Acute Sound Stress," *Mol. Cell Neurosci.* 5(2):176–181.

37. C.L. Melchior and R.F. Ritzman. 1994. "Dehydroepiandrosterone is an Anxiolytic in Mice on the Plus Maze," *Pharmacol. Biochem. Behav.* 47(3):437–441.

38. S.M. Haffner, R.A. Valdez, L. Mykkanen, M.P. Stern, M.S. Katz. 1994. "Decreased Testosterone and Dehydroandrosterone Sulfate Concentrations Are Associated with Increased Insulin and Glucose Concentrations in Nondiabetic Men," *Metabolism* 43(5):599–603.

39. L.F. Berkman, T.E. Seeman, M. Albert, D. Blazer, R. Kahn, R. Mohs, C. Finch, E. Schneider, C. Cotman and G. McClearn. 1993. "High, Usual and Impaired Functioning in Community-Dwelling Older Men and Women: Findings from

the MacArthur Foundation Research Network on Successful Aging," *J. Clin. Epidemiol.* 46(10):1129–1140.

40. D. L. Coleman, E. H. Leiter and N. Applezweig. 1984. "Therapeutic Effects of Dehydroepiandrosterone Metabolites in Diabetic Mice, (c57BL/KsJ-db/db)," *Endocrinology* 115:239–243.

41. M.P. Cleary, T. Zabel and J. L. Sartin. 1988. "Effects of Short-Term Dehydroepiandrosterone Treatment on Serum and Pancreatic Insulin in Zucker Rats," *J. Nutr.* 118:382–387.

42. G. E. MacEwen and I.D. Kurzman. 1991. "Obesity in the Dog: Role of the Adrenal Steroid Dehydroepiandrosterone (DHEA)," *J. Nutr.* 121:S51–S55.

43. I.D. Kurzman, E. G. MacEwen and A. L. M. Haffa. 1990. "Reduction in the Body Weight and Cholesterol in Spontaneously Obese Dogs by Dehydroepiandrosterone," *Int. J. Obesity* 14:95–104.

44. J.E. Nestler, C. O. Barlascini, J. N. Clore and W. G. Blackard. 1988. "Dehydroepiandrosterone Reduces Serum Low Density Lipoprotein Levels and Body Fat but Does Not Alter Insulin Sensitivity in Normal Men," *J. Clin Endocrinol. & Metab.* 66:57–61.

45. P.F. Mohan and M.P. Cleary. 1989. "Comparison of Dehydroepiandrosterone and Clofibric Acid Treatments in Obese Zucker Rats," *J. Nutr.* 119:496–501.

46. D. J. Jakubowicz, N.A. Beer, R.M. Beer and J. E. Nestler, "Disparate Effects of Weight Reduction by Diet on Serum Dehydroepiandrosterone-Sulfate Levels in Obese Men and Women," Dehydroepiandrosterone (DHEA) and Aging, New York Academy of Sciences Meeting, June 17–19, 1995.

47. O.M. Wolkowitz, V.I. Reus, E. Roberts, F. Manfredi, T. Chan, S. Ormiston, R. Johnson, J. Canick, L. Brizedine and H. Weingartner, "Antidepressant and Cognition-Enhancing Effects of DHEA in Major Depression," Dehydroepiandrosterone (DHEA) and Aging, New York Academy of Sciences Meeting, June 17–19, 1995.